The OATH OF LOVE

DAILY INSPIRATIONAL JOURNAL FOR COUPLES

MAGAN J. & OMAR PARSONS

The OATH OF LOVE

DAILY INSPIRATIONAL JOURNAL FOR COUPLES

MAGAN J. & OMAR PARSONS

GEMLIGHT
PUBLISHING LLC

FORT WORTH, TEXAS

Copyright © 2024 by Magan & Omar Parsons

All rights reserved.

No part of this book may be reproduced in any form without written permission from the publisher or author, except as permitted by U.S. copyright law.

This publication is designed to provide accurate and authoritative information regarding the subject matter covered. It is sold with the understanding that neither the author nor the publisher is engaged in rendering legal, investment, accounting, or other professional services. While the publisher and author have used their best efforts in preparing this book, they make no representations or warranties with respect to the accuracy or completeness of the contents of this book and specifically disclaim any implied warranties of merchantability or fitness for a particular purpose. No warranty may be created or extended by sales representatives or written sales materials. The advice and strategies contained herein may not be suitable for your situation. You should consult with a professional when appropriate. Neither the publisher nor the author shall be liable for any loss of profit or any other commercial damages, including but not limited to special, incidental, consequential, personal, or other damages.

Scripture quotations, unless otherwise indicated, are taken from the Holy Bible, New International Version®, NIV®. Copyright ©1973, 1978, 1984, 2011 by Biblica, Inc.™ Used by permission of Zondervan. All rights reserved worldwide. www.zondervan.comThe "NIV" and "New International Version" are trademarks registered in the United States Patent and Trademark Office by Biblica, Inc.™

Scripture quotations are from the ESV® Bible (The Holy Bible, English Standard Version®), copyright © 2001 by Crossway Bibles, a publishing ministry of Good News Publishers. Used by permission. All rights reserved."

ISBN: 979-8-8693-0735-4
Printed in the United States of America
Publisher: Gemlight Publishing LLC
9500 Ray White Rd, Ste 200
Fort Worth. Texas 76244
817-745-4556
www.gemlightpublishiing.com

Foreword ......

In the beginning, on Earth, Adam was alone and God set forth to make a help meet, and they became one
(Genesis 2:18).
Even in the beginning of the Earth, the Devil tried to become between the man and woman, and deceive the woman. As Ecclesiastes 1:9 states:

"What has been will be again,
what has been done will be done again;
there is nothing new under the sun."

Which sums it up: nothing is new; as we go through life trying to create this "perfect" relationship or marriage—we should wake up and know—it will not happen! There will be bad days, then good days, that is why the Word was created, and God should be the center of your Love.

As you read this journal and follow along with the guides, scriptures, and activities, we want you to understand that being friends with one another is the center of a healthy marriage. Often couples are together—and do not like one another! Can you *love* someone and not *like* them? YES! Ninety-nine percent of the time couples join and have a past of being hurt by someone. So, we go through life trying to find the quick fix remedy. The relationship starts off amazing, then great, then good, then okay, then all right, then it will get better, then separation, then divorce. So, the questions are: what are these phases? And what are you doing to stop you both from drowning?

As you sincerely join into a relationship, it's an OATH! You will have waves of challenges, tests of misunderstandings, and a rollercoaster of uncertainty; however, the bond of agreement is with a profound emphasis on spirituality, and the transformative power of a God-centered union.

The Oath of Love will help reinforce the foundations of love, trust, and faith, fostering a lasting and fulfilling partnership.

If you are in a couple looking to live in a healthy and thriving relationship, then this is the *right* book for you.

Now let us dive in.

Table of Contents

WHY WE LOVE 9
- Day 1 11
- Day 2 15
- Day 3 19

REASONS WHY WE LOVE 23
- Day 4 25
- Day 5 29
- Day 6 33
- Day 7 37
- Day 8 41
- Day 9 45
- Day 10 51
- Day 11 55
- Day 12 59
- Day 13 63

THE POWER OF LOVE 67
- Day 14 69
- Day 15 73
- Day 16 77
- Day 17 81
- Day 18 85
- Day 19 89
- Day 20 93
- Day 21 97
- Day 22 101
- Day 23 105
- Day 24 109
- Day 25 113

WHY WE LOVE

Day 1

Uncovering the Roots of Deep Attachment in Our Relationship

"Love is something that should be valued, a feeling that is not easily broken. At all times God should be the source and foundation of the love you have, want, or even desire. How can we as people truly love with God, when the Bible simply states, "God is love". Whoever lives in love, lives in God, and God in him—1 John 4:8. With a family relationship or marriage, loving someone for real should be your goal.

Love aloud, love boldly, love publicly, and privately. Show people that *true* love exists. A love does not hurt you, wound you, or scar you. I have a question: do you love yourself?? If the answer to my question is "no", I want you to know that you cannot love anyone else if you don´t love yourself.

We go through things that break us, relationships, TRAUMA as a child, loss of someone who was, or is currently, dear to our heart. Being hurt or mishandled can cause us to fall *out of love* with others, as well as ourself. Heal first, so that you can love *again* and receive a true and real love, like no other.

Love is an enchanting symphony that resonates within the depths of our souls. It transcends the boundaries of time and space, weaving a tapestry of emotions, connections, and understanding that binds hearts together. At its core, love is an unwavering acceptance of someone for who they truly are—embracing both their strengths and vulnerabilities. It is the profound ability to see beauty in imperfection, and in doing so, to *find* perfection in the uniqueness of everyone.

Love is a nurturing force that inspires growth, and encourages us to be the *best* version of ourselves. It empowers us to face our fears, break down walls, and open ourselves up to vulnerability, knowing that in each other's presence, we are safe. It is a gentle touch that ignites a thousand sparks, a warm embrace that provides solace during life's storms, and a reassuring smile that speaks a thousand unspoken words.

Love is not merely an emotion; it is a verb, a conscious choice to care, support, and uplift one another. It is an unselfish act of putting someone else's happiness before our own, rejoicing in their triumphs, and sharing their burdens. In love, we find a profound sense of belonging—a home within another's heart. It is a sanctuary where we can be fully seen, understood, and loved for our true selves. Love is patient and kind, forgiving and compassionate. It endures the trials and tribulations that life may present, standing firm like an ancient oak tree, weathering the storms while growing *ever* stronger.

Yet—love is not without its challenges.

The Mindset Behind Our Relationships

How exactly do you love? Do you say that you are "in love" with someone but show it? We all have diverse ways of showing and receiving love, the old folks call them love languages. Some may want money as a love language, some may want gifts and cards, some may want to go on a romantic date, some may not care if you spend time with them, or they have someone that they can call their own.

How do you love? And what is your love language? These questions you should be asking yourself figure out, so when the time comes, and your mate finds you, you will know what you want, and how to display it.

A healthy relationship/marriage must know these things—they are important. Love is a beautiful thing/feeling when you *know* your partner and want what *they* need and require. Most relationships/marriages never work because the two never agree, and never take the time to truly get to know one another. How can two walk together, unless they agree.

Your mind, as it enters an intimate relationship, knows love is only a word until you make it something special with another person. Look at it as a policy with no terms and conditions. When we enter into intimacy and share the love language with our partners, we are not then warning ourselves about the outcome of the way our love will grow.

The mindset behind our most intimate relationships is a multifaceted and complex topic. It encompasses a wide range of factors, including emotional intelligence, attachment styles, and subjective experiences. Our mindset significantly influences the way we approach and engage in intimate relationships, shaping the dynamics, longevity, and overall satisfaction we derive from them.

One crucial aspect of the mindset behind intimate relationships is emotional intelligence. Emotional intelligence refers to the ability to be aware of, understand, and manage our own emotions—and those of others. When applied to intimate relationships, emotional intelligence allows individuals to communicate effectively, show empathy, and make deeper connections.

People with high emotional intelligence tend to be more attuned to their partner's needs and feelings, fostering a sense of closeness and emotional safety. They are better equipped to interpret and respond to cues, avoiding misunderstandings and conflicts. Additionally, emotional intelligence enables individuals to express their emotions clearly and constructively, creating an environment where vulnerability and authenticity thrive.

Our heart deceives us sometimes, so when you say you love a person, you have to make sure it is true, real, and from God.

I encourage you to know and hear the voice of God.

Day 3

Easy to Say LOVE?

Love can be easily understood if one is willing to be transparent about it, which is an open book if you allow it to be. Love comes with a lot of give and take, back and forth, agree to disagree-type vibes. True love opens doors for communication for things to be said that people/couples never feel/felt like they were able to say, or bring up. Love at times can be so deep, yet so simple. Love sets and shifts all atmospheres for people to love, and in return *receive* love, as well as it allows everything to flow like it is supposed to.

What exactly do you think love is? It is not just a look, or feeling, or action—but love is indeed a *standard*. Standard means a level of quality or attainment.

Yeah, I know that was good, right?!? We have seen love for what it is worth, not what it *is*. Love allows other things in life to flow without restrictions in peace, joy, and happiness. Learn to love with no regrets. For the times you thought you were in love, and it turned out to be lust, learn from that, so that you will never make that same mistake again. Love comes in many forms, but the question is: are you open to the things that *do not* appear the way you think they should?

Love is a word that is often used casually, and without much thought. It is thrown around in conversations and appears in countless song lyrics and poetry. But, is it easy to say "love"?

The concept of love is complex and multifaceted, encompassing a wide range of emotions, actions, and experiences. Love can mean different things to different individuals, and it can manifest in various forms such as romantic love, familial love, or platonic love. It goes beyond a mere four-letter word and delves into the deepest reaches of human emotion.

Primarily, love requires vulnerability. When we love someone, we open ourselves up to the possibility of being hurt or rejected. It takes courage to let our guard down and expose our innermost feelings to another person. We risk being disappointed or betrayed—yet we still *choose to love* because it brings joy, connection, and fulfillment to our lives.

Additionally, love demands selflessness. It is not simply about receiving affection or attention but giving it freely and unconditionally. Love requires us to put *someone else's* needs and desires above our own. It means being empathetic, compassionate, and understanding. Love is about constantly striving to support and uplift those we care about—even when it is not convenient or easy.

Love is also a commitment. It is not a fleeting emotion that comes and goes; rather, it is a choice we make every day. Love requires effort, patience, and dedication. It is not always glamorous or easy, but it is *worth* fighting for.

REASONS WHY WE LOVE

Day 51

An Exploration of the Reasons We Care Deeply for Our Partners

Love can be so magical, and love can be mysterious.
Mysterious—difficult, or impossible to understand. Magical—beautiful or delightful. So, with love you can have the best of both worlds, you just have to know *who* to love and *how* to love them.

Prepare for the kind of love you wish to have. Love is so strong and powerful that it can save a broken relationship, it can stop a divorce—or make one happen. Love can also have you stuck in a place that you should not be.

Please understand the difference between a good love and a bad one. "Good" meaning happy, healthy, and on one accord. "Bad" meaning sad, broken, hurt, or toxic. Know the difference not only for relationships or marriage, but this goes for everything, everyone, and all situations.

I am writing this journal because I have had my share of both good and bad. Right now, the only love I want to experience is a good one full of fun, joy, and laughter. We must understand the reasons we start caring for our partner and eventually fell in love. Was it at the most vulnerable time in your life? Were they the only person there to listen, hug or *be* there? Or was it a moment you were going to give up on love, but things happened that put you two together. Whatever it is we care deeply for them, and this leads to love. Often, we can love things a person does, but not care for them, which can get you confused with just lust.

There are five levels of Love:

Level 1—LIKING

This is the level when you like someone by sharing similar social status and having things in common.

Level 2—AFFECTIONS
This level is when you are spending quality time together, and continuing to bond and connect, and affection and emotions will unsurprisingly develop. Many people stay in this level and never get to the next level of commitment.

Level 3—RESTRICTED COMMITMENTS
The level when you love them for who they are, not for what they *have*, however, only if they show you the same love back. You have grown to trust them on a restricted level.

Level 4—UNRESTRICTED COMMITMENTS
On this level, everything is all in the open. All the baggage of the past, secrets are told and you 100% still love them. You are ready to commit, for better or worse, and you say, "We, Bonnie and Clyde!" It is when they want and need something they become your priority.

Level 5—SACRIFICIAL LOVE
This level is only visible if you achieve level 4 and stick with it. It is the level of love that when you have been mistreated, you still love; when you show all the love toward them in actions, and you never get anything in return—financially, sexually or mentally.

You are on a one-way street in the relationship. It's not the level everyone would typically like to give. When they have proven themselves untrustworthy and you *still* are faithful to them.

Often in relationships people jump ship if things become difficult, and give no room to deepen their love in the relationship. If God would love us all on the level of 1 and 3 do you think he would bring his son to die on the cross for our sins? The answer is NO!!

So, dealing with love, we must understand the levels.

Day 5

How We Can Find Fulfillment and Joy in Our Partners

True love goes through a process and development to be effective. It takes hard work and "dedication". That word means the quality of being dedicated or committed to a task or purpose. Often, we cannot find true love because we do not know what to look for. There must be a sense of joy in the relationship for you to go into the love process. You must find what leads you to joy—even through the toughest times in the relationship, and to build on it. Whatever we do in life, we build from habits to become consistently "normal" for us. You have invested the time to make your relationship happier, and create an atmosphere you are comfortable feeling.

Remember, happiness makes your brain work better!

Finding fulfillment and joy in our partners is an integral part of building a healthy and fulfilling relationship. In today's fast-paced and often chaotic world, it can be easy to overlook the importance of nurturing these aspects of our relationships. However, with conscious effort and understanding, we can create *lasting* happiness and find true contentment in our partnership.

Effective communication is the foundation of a fulfilling relationship. It involves active listening, expressing thoughts and feelings honestly, and being open to understanding our partner's perspective. Transparent communication allows couples to build trust and deepen their connection, enhancing the joy and fulfillment they find in each other's company.

Other crucial aspects are acceptance, and unconditional love. We are all unique individuals with our own strengths, weaknesses, and quirks. Embracing and celebrating our partner's individuality creates a sense of security and allows them to flourish, without judgment or criticism. This acceptance enables us to find joy in the journey of growth and self-discovery with our partners, cultivating a sense of fulfillment and deepening our love for each other.

Finding fulfillment and joy in our relationship with our partners is a continuous journey that requires conscious effort, effective communication, acceptance, and support. By prioritizing quality time, expressing appreciation, and encouraging personal growth, we can create a solid foundation for a healthy and fulfilling relationship. When both partners invest in nurturing their connection, they can experience lasting happiness, and find genuine contentment in each other's presence.

Day 6

Discovering the Meaning of True Love in Our Relationships

True love hurts, but it would never drag you through the mud, nor would it belittle you in any way. True love would not appear to only love you in private, and never public. True would not hurt you intentionally. We all deserve a love that is pure and not contaminated. Love can be a way out for you, in so many ways. It can be the key to unlock things that you felt hurt by, and was never able to discuss or talk about.

True love is essential for a healthy and fulfilling relationship that is built on trust, companionship, and the ability to overcome obstacles together.

True love is founded on trust, honesty, and deep emotional connection. It is not merely a physical attraction or infatuation, but rather a genuine affection and care for one another's well-being. True love involves putting the needs of your partner before your own, supporting each other through thick and thin, and celebrating each other's successes.

One key aspect of true love in a relationship is accepting your partner for who they truly are. This means embracing their flaws and imperfections and loving them— unconditionally. True love means supporting each other in personal growth and allowing each other the space to be individuals within the relationship.

In a relationship characterized by true love, communication is essential. Open and honest communication is the foundation for understanding and resolving conflicts. It involves active listening, empathy, and a willingness to compromise. True love entails being vulnerable and expressing your feelings, needs, and desires without fear of judgment or rejection.

Another essential element of true love in a relationship is mutual respect. This means valuing each other's opinions, boundaries, and personal space. True love involves treating your partner with kindness, empathy, and respect—even in moments of disagreement or frustration. It is about recognizing that you are two separate individuals with different perspectives—still choosing to love and respect each other.

Day 7

A Look at the Painful Side of Love

People say love does not hurt, but the truth is—it can and does. Especially when someone says that they love you, or have your back, but show you otherwise. They might show that what they said and who they pretended to be was *not* true. Be careful, because some people can notice your pain and your hurt, and they come on pretending to be the one who loves you, but the whole time all they wanted to do was *break you down* even more. This was the demonic assignment set out against you, so this is why I said earlier make sure your heart is not being deceitful. Some people put faces on well, they look the part—but intentions can be completely off the charts.

One of the most painful aspects of love is rejection. When we love someone and they do not reciprocate our feelings, it can feel like a dagger through the heart. The pain of unrequited love can be excruciating, leaving us feeling worthless and unlovable. We may question our self-worth and wonder what is wrong with us, leading to feelings of depression and despair. The ache of rejection can linger for weeks, months, or even years, leaving a lasting scar on our hearts.

Another painful side of love is heartbreak. When a relationship that we have invested time, energy, and emotions into ends—it can feel like our world is crashing down. The pain of losing a loved one can be overwhelming, leaving us feeling empty and shattered. We may experience physical symptoms such as loss of appetite, insomnia, and even physical pain. Heartbreak can leave us feeling disillusioned and cynical about love, affecting our ability to trust and open up to others in the future.

Furthermore, love can also bring about feelings of jealousy and possessiveness, which can be incredibly painful. When we love someone deeply, the thought of them being with someone else can send us into a spiral of insecurity and anguish. Jealousy can fuel irrational behavior, leading to toxic relationships and even emotional or physical abuse. The pain of jealousy can consume us, causing us to lose our sense of self and become obsessed with controlling our partner's actions.

Love is a complex and multifaceted emotion that brings both joy and pain. While we often focus on the positive aspects of love, it is essential to recognize and address the painful side. Rejection, heartbreak, jealousy, and unmet expectations are some of the painful experiences that can arise from loving someone. By acknowledging and understanding these aspects, we can navigate love more consciously and create healthier relationships. Love is not *perfect*, but by embracing its painful side, we can grow and learn from our experiences, finding deeper and more fulfilling connections with others.

Day 8

Evaluating your Heart to Love.

John 13: 34-35—A new commandment I give to you: that ye love one another as I have loved you; that ye also love one another. By this shall men know about God´s love.

Many of us do not know about this type of love, because when it comes to others, we are way too selfish. We talk down on the ones we say we love/care about, rather than do what God has commanded us to do. When will we become a people who love without any strings attached? We need to check our heart and ask ourselves this question: Do I really love others the way that *I* want to be loved? What has you thinking that you *deserve* a love, a love that you cannot give in return. Love is a profound, complex emotion that binds us to others. It has the power to bring immense joy, happiness, and fulfillment into our lives. However, it is crucial that we examine our own hearts when expressing love towards others. By doing so, we can ensure that our actions are genuine, sincere, and compassionate, rather than driven by selfish motives, or personal gain. We need to understand the importance of self-reflection, and checking our heart in cultivating healthy, nurturing relationships based on love. This leads to these five evaluations:

1. Self-Mindfulness:
Before entering any relationship, it is vital to examine our motives and feelings. Understanding our true intentions is essential, to avoid entering relationships for superficial reasons, or ulterior motives. By practicing self-awareness, we can recognize our own flaws, biases, and emotional needs, leading to more genuine connections with others.

2. Compassion:
Genuine love encompasses empathy and compassion. It is crucial to care about the emotions and well-being of others, and prioritize their

needs without expecting anything in return. When we check our hearts, we ensure that our love is not driven by selfish desires but by a sincere intention to support and uplift those around us.

3. Respect and Boundaries:
Respecting the boundaries and autonomy of others is a crucial aspect of loving relationships. We should never impose our ideas, ambitions, or desires on someone else without considering *their* feelings and values. Checking our hearts allows us to navigate relationships with humility and respect.

4. Emotional Availability:
Being emotionally available is a key factor in fostering healthy relationships. By checking our hearts, we can address any unresolved emotional baggage or past traumas that may hinder our ability to give and receive love. Only when we are emotionally healthy and available can we truly engage in meaningful connections.

5. Unconditional Love:
Unconditional love requires selflessness and acceptance. It means loving someone *just as* they are, without expecting them to change or conform to our ideals. By checking our hearts, we evaluate whether we can offer unwavering support and affection, even in tough times or when facing challenges.

By practicing self-awareness, empathy, and respect, we can foster genuine connections and build healthy relationships with those around us. Ultimately, checking our hearts allows us to create a nurturing and loving environment where all individuals are valued and celebrated for who they truly are.

Day 9

Overcoming Contaminated Love

Sometimes, it can simply be *hard* to love the people you truly care about. I say that because some of us just do not know how it feels to receive a healthy love, we are so used to the toxic love, the love that breaks you, and does not build you—the love that brings much sadness, with no happiness. We have become a people who are used to, and comfortable with, loving or being in love with someone we *should not*.

In times like these, you must pray for direction from God, to show you who you should be in love with. Loving everyone? Yes, you are supposed to. But please know it is OK to let go of a love that does not push you to be a better person. Sometimes we hold on because we do not think the love we truly deserve will ever appear. Think along these lines: *I am ordered to receive the love God has for me, but if he tells me to let go of something or someone, then I will do that.*

Do not be greedy trying to have everything. Love comes with much disappointment, but it depends on what you are willing to accept in your life as real love, true love, and authentic love. Love is a transforming and multifaceted emotion that will bring immense joy and fulfillment, but it can also have a dark side. Sometimes, love becomes contaminated, tainted by toxicity, manipulation, and abuse. However, it is crucial that individuals recognize and address these issues to overcome contaminated love and safeguard their well-being.

1. Understanding contaminated love:
Contaminated love is characterized by unhealthy dynamics and patterns that negatively affect one's mental and emotional well-being. It often includes elements of control, manipulation, abuse, dishonesty, and lack of respect. Contaminated love can come in various forms, such as romantic relationships, friendships, or even

familial ties. It erodes self-esteem, distorts feeling, and stifles personal growth.

2. Recognizing the signs:
It is crucial to see the signs of contaminated love to address the issue effectively.

3. Breaking free from contaminated love:
Overcoming contaminated love requires a steadfast commitment to one's own well-being and personal growth.

Here are some strategies to consider:

a. Self-reflection: Start by introspecting and understanding personal values, desires, and boundaries. This self-awareness helps in recognizing the disparities between what love should be, and what it has become.

b. Seek support: Reach out to trusted friends, family members, or professionals who can provide objective perspectives and emotional support. Surrounding oneself with positive influences helps rebuild damaged self-esteem and proves a support network during challenging times.

c. Establish boundaries: Clearly define and communicate personal boundaries to protect oneself emotionally and physically. Enforcing boundaries provides a sense of control, and prevents others from crossing lines that perpetuate toxic dynamics.

d. Redefine self-worth: It is crucial to recognize one's inherent value and worth, independent of any tainted relationships. Engaging in self-care activities, affirmations, and therapy helps rebuild self-esteem and confidence.

e. Cut ties if necessary: In extreme situations, it may be necessary to sever ties completely to safeguard emotional and physical well-being. Exiting a toxic relationship is a bold step towards reclaiming happiness and moving towards healthier connections.

Overcoming contaminated love is a challenging journey that demands courage, self-reflection, and resilience, which can only be fulfilled by having a relationship with God.

When Love Goes Wrong

Have you ever heard that saying, "Hurt people hurt people." Hurt people do not, or will not know how to live until they heal. I have had many experiences with hurt people being able to love, but all they really do is hurt others.

In the church you have leaders in positions who are hurt, both male and female, and yet all they do is hurt everyone they come in contact with, because they are hurt themselves. I have experienced this in jobs where people are in places of leadership and power, and they use that to abuse others, because they are so broken and hurt. So, before you get into those positions, and before you can love anyone, pray and ask God to heal and mend your broken heart. Because you will be held accountable for hurting those God has sent for you to love. We must learn the true meaning of love, and begin to do so.

It is essential to address the pain and hurt that individuals carry to break this cycle. Hurt people need support, understanding, and compassion to heal from their past traumas. They need to know that their pain does not *define* them, and that they can still find love and happiness. With therapy, self-reflection, and the support of loved ones, individuals can learn healthier ways to process their emotions, and cope with their pain. By facing their own suffering, they can break free from the cycle of hurt and begin to build healthier, more fulfilling relationships.

Love gone wrong is a tragic and unfortunate reality in our lives. It has the power to turn individuals into hurt people who, in turn, hurt others. However, it is important for us, as a society, to recognize the interconnectedness of our emotions and behavior. By addressing the pain and trauma that exists within us, we can break free from the cycle of hurt, and create a more loving and compassionate world.

The pain and trauma experienced in relationships can lead individuals to project their suffering onto others. It is essential for us as individuals and as a society to provide support and healing for those who have been hurt, to break that cycle of hurt, and create more loving and healthy relationships.

Finding Hope in Heartache

I love some folk, despite them hurting me and breaking me down; despite them backstabbing me and talking about it I still had to love them. That hurts more than anything, but it is in that *very* moment that you find out who you really are, and what you truly stand for.

Loving everyone is not *easy*, but it is our job to forgive and to love *no matter* what has been done. Doing this helps you live freely and not bound to the hurt, disappointment and betrayal, the setbacks as well as the set-ups people have done or are doing to you. Learn to forgive so that you can love again.

Finding love after heartache can be a frightening and vulnerable experience. It requires us to take a leap of faith, to trust ourselves and others again. But hope provides us with a safety net, assuring us that we are not alone on this journey. It gives us the confidence to put ourselves out there, to take a chance on love again.

When we finally decide to open our hearts to love once more, hope is there every step of the way. It guides us in choosing healthy relationships, encouraging us to be patient and discerning. It helps us to let go of past hurts and fears, allowing us to fully embrace the possibilities that lie ahead.

In the end, finding *hope* in heartache allows us to love again. It teaches us that heartbreak is not the end of our story, but merely a chapter in the grand narrative of our lives. Hope reminds us that love is a beautiful and transformative force that can heal our wounds and ignite our souls.

So, dear friend, when faced with heartache, take a deep breath, and let hope be your compass. Embrace the pain, heal, and find the *strength* to love again. For, in the pursuit of love, hope is the guiding light that will lead you to a future filled with joy, happiness, and endless possibilities.

Day 12

Boss Up and Express Your Feelings of Love

The word "love" simply means caring a lot. Some people are "in love" with others, and you think it is just a matter of you caring for them. If you know you have feelings for someone, or are in love with someone, please do not be afraid to tell them. Life is too short to love someone and them not even *know* your love existed for them. So, if you are reading this and you have feelings for, care for, or are in love with someone—please tell them. Loving from a pure place is indeed what the world lacks today.

Love is a powerful emotion that can transform lives, heal wounds, and uplift spirits. Unfortunately, expressing feelings of love is often accompanied by uncertainties, fear of rejection, and societal norms that dictate how and when one should convey one's emotions. However, by assuming a fearless and confident attitude, it is possible to "boss up" and express your feelings of love, thereby opening the doors to a world of joy and fulfillment.

Understand the ways to express your love interest.

1. Embrace vulnerability:
To express feelings of love, one must embrace vulnerability. It requires setting aside the fear of being hurt or rejected and opening oneself up to the possibility of reciprocation. Acknowledge that expressing love is not a sign of weakness, but rather an act of strength, as it reveals the depth of your emotions and your willingness to take risks for the sake of love.

2. Communicate openly and honestly:
Communication is the key to any successful relationship. Expressing love necessitates creating a safe space where open and honest conversations can take place. Clearly and calmly articulate your feelings while ensuring that you respect the other person's boundaries and emotions. It is important to express love with authenticity, as

forced or insincere expressions may lead to misunderstandings or hurt feelings.

3. Overcome the fear of rejection:
One obstacle that often holds individuals back from expressing their love is the fear of rejection. However, it is crucial to remember that rejection is a natural part of life. By understanding that rejection is not a reflection of your self-worth, but rather a mismatch of emotions or circumstances, you can approach love with a more positive perspective. Embrace rejection as an opportunity for personal growth, and learn from the experience.

4. Choose the right moment:
Timing is everything when it comes to expressing love. While it is important to be honest and open, it is equally crucial to choose the right moment. Consider the other person's emotional state, the context of the situation, and ensure that they are receptive to your feelings. By selecting a good and opportune moment, it increases the chances of a positive and meaningful interaction.

5. Be prepared for various outcomes:
Expressing one's love does not always guarantee a positive outcome; however, it is essential to be prepared for all scenarios. While rejection may initially sting, try to keep your grace and respect for the other person's decision. Understanding that their feelings may change over time or that it simply *was not meant to be* is crucial. Regardless of the outcome, expressing love shows authenticity, courage, and self-awareness.

We must remember to communicate openly and honestly, overcome the fear of rejection, choose the right moment, and be prepared for various outcomes. Ultimately, expressing love is an empowering experience that can lead to deeper connections, personal growth, and the good chance of finding reciprocated affection. So, boss up and express your feelings of love, and may it pave the way for a life filled with joy, passion, and meaningful relationships!

Day By

Unlocking Mature Love

A mature love is one that is stable, one that's kind, one that forgives, one that trusts, one that can make yourself—as well as everyone around you—happy.

A mature love is free and not forced. A forced love can end up being a failed love. Love someone who you can love every day, no matter the problem or situation. We do not need a love that is wishy-washy, and only wants to love when things are going well.

Mature love goes beyond the superficial aspects of physical attraction or fleeting romantic notions. It is a deep-rooted connection that exists on the level of the soul, transcending the boundaries of time and physical appearances. This type of love is nurtured through shared experiences, mutual respect, and unwavering commitment. Mature love understands that love is not always a bed of roses. It requires effort, compromise, and the ability to weather storms together.

In a relationship, mature love displays an openness and vulnerability that allows for genuine growth and understanding. It acknowledges the flaws and imperfections of both individuals and loves without judgment or unrealistic expectations. It is rooted in acceptance, recognizing that no person is flawless and that it is through one's limitations that true strength can be found. This love is patient and steadfast, willing to stand by partners through the darkest of times.

This love is not built on self-serving desires but on a genuine desire to see the other person flourish and find fulfillment. This love values the growth and happiness of the other individual as much as its own.

Mature love is patient, steadfast, and willing to stand by partners through thick and thin. It evolves and adapts, recognizing the importance of personal growth within the relationship. In a world that often celebrates fleeting and superficial relationships, it is the mature love that stands out as the true manifestation of deep human connection and emotional maturity.

THE POWER OF LOVE

Day IH

Weathering the Storm

I find myself reflecting on the times we have weathered storms in our relationship. Just like unpredictable weather, life has thrown challenges our way, but through it all, we have stood together, and become stronger than ever. The storms we faced were not always easy to navigate. There were difficult times of uncertainty, doubt, and fear, but with each storm that passed, we developed a deeper understanding of each other and a renewed sense of resilience. In the face of adversity, our love proved its strength. We learned to communicate openly, listening to each other's concerns and fears with compassion and empathy. Together, we faced turbulent emotions and found solace in knowing that we were not *alone* in this journey.

During those storms, we held onto each other, providing support and reassurance. We found comfort in the mere presence of one another, knowing that love can be a sturdy anchor amidst the chaos of life. Our commitment to weathering these storms together grew stronger, and our bond deepened as a result. We also learned valuable lessons from facing those challenges. These trials tested our patience and taught us the art of compromise. We discovered that by working together as a team, we could overcome *any* obstacle that life throws our way.

Weathering a storm, navigating the difficulties of love, requires resilience, patience, and a solid foundation. Just as storms bring chaos and uncertainty, love can sometimes feel quite overwhelming and tumultuous. However, it is in weathering these storms that relationships do grow stronger, and the individuals within them find their true strength.

One of the first challenges of love is the initial storm of emotions that often goes with it. Love has a way of stirring up intense feelings—from euphoria and passion, to insecurity and vulnerability.

These emotions can feel overwhelming sometimes, leaving individuals feeling lost and unsure of how to navigate through them. Like a storm, these feelings can make it difficult to see clearly and make rational decisions. It is during these times that communication and self-reflection become essential. Open and honest communication allows partners to navigate through their emotions together, supporting each other along the way.

Love can bring external storms that also test the strength of a relationship. Life is unpredictable, and circumstances beyond our control can affect our relationships. These storms can range from financial hardship to the loss of loved ones, and they can leave individuals feeling devastated and vulnerable. However, coping in these storms together can foster a deeper connection and understanding between partners. It is during these trying times that the true strength of a relationship is revealed, and support and love become fundamental. By standing together and facing external obstacles head-on, couples can emerge stronger, and more resilient. With open communication, empathy, and a commitment to facing the low points together, love can grow stronger, and individuals can find their true strength. Just as stormy weather clears to reveal a bright sky, love can emerge even *stronger* and more beautiful after weathering the inevitable storms.

Day 15

Power of Vulnerability

At first, opening up and exposing my deepest feelings felt quite daunting, but as we both embraced vulnerability, our connection deepened in ways I never imagined possible. In moments of vulnerability, we found solace and support, knowing we could lean on each other without judgment or fear. Sharing our fears and insecurities brought us closer, and it was through vulnerability that we learned to understand and cherish each other's vulnerabilities.

Being vulnerable allowed us to break down walls and barriers, creating a safe space where honesty and authenticity thrive. It strengthened our emotional intimacy, and I came to realize that true intimacy lies in being seen and accepted for our *whole* selves. Our vulnerability also taught us to communicate openly and honestly, leading to more profound conversations and a deeper emotional bond. Through these heartfelt exchanges, we found resolution, and were able to thrive in the face of challenges.

Many people are often led to believe that vulnerability is a sign of weakness, that it makes one susceptible to harm or rejection. However, the truth is that vulnerability is an immense source of strength, courage, and intimacy in a relationship. It is through vulnerability that individuals can cultivate trust, deepen connections, and foster personal growth. By embracing vulnerability, partners can create a safe and authentic space for emotional expression, leading to a more fulfilling and meaningful relationship.

Vulnerability is the act of opening oneself up to another person, baring our true selves without fear of judgment or rejection. It requires a level of honesty and emotional exposure that can be challenging—and uncomfortable. Yet, it is precisely this vulnerability that paves the way for genuine intimacy and growth in a relationship.

Primarily, vulnerability is at the core of building trust. Trust is the foundation upon which any healthy relationship is built. When individuals are willing to be vulnerable, they are saying, "I trust you with my authentic self." By being honest and open, they are taking a leap of faith, trusting their partner to hold and cherish their vulnerabilities. This mutual vulnerability creates a strong bond of trust, as both partners feel safe enough to reveal their true selves without fear of judgment or betrayal.

While vulnerability carries immense power, it is important to note that it must be practiced in a safe and supportive environment. Both partners must be committed to creating a judgment-free space where vulnerabilities are embraced, not exploited. It is crucial to approach vulnerability in a relationship with empathy, understanding, and respect for one another's boundaries.

Day 16

God in Marriage

From the very beginning of our journey together, we felt an connection that defied explanation—a sense of destiny that guided us towards each other. As we travelled along the difficult paths of life, our faith in God has been a steadfast anchor, providing comfort, wisdom, and strength during the toughest times. God has blessed us with moments of joy and celebration, reminding us that love is a gift to cherish and nurture. In times of challenge and disagreement, we turn to our shared beliefs to find forgiveness and understanding. Our shared spiritual connection has allowed us to grow and learn together, fostering an environment of love, respect, and compassion. In our marriage, we have learned to rely on prayer and seek guidance from God in making important decisions. We trust that He will lead us on the right path and grant us the wisdom to face whatever comes our way. I am grateful for a partner who not only loves and supports me unconditionally, but also shares a deep spiritual bond with me. Together, we draw strength from our faith, and are reminded that through God's grace our marriage is alive, growing and resilient.

One of the central roles God offers in marriage is providing guidance and wisdom. Marriage is a dynamic relationship that requires constant effort and compromise. There are moments of joy, but also challenges and conflicts that every couple must face. In times of difficulty, turning to God can provide the necessary wisdom and discernment to keep afloat through the storm. By seeking His guidance, couples can find answers to their dilemmas and make informed decisions that will strengthen their bond. The belief in a Divine power brings comfort and assurance that there is a *higher purpose* for their union.

God in marriage brings a greater sense of purpose and meaning. Marriage is not merely a legal or social contract; it is a covenant built on love, sacrifice, and commitment. The belief in a Divine plan for marriage instills a deep understanding of the *significance* of this commitment. It encourages couples to nurture and cultivate their relationship, realizing that their union has a greater purpose beyond their individual happiness. This shared purpose can help couples remain focused on the long-term goals of their marriage, and make the necessary sacrifices for the sake of their mutual growth and well-being.

However, it is important to note that the inclusion of God in marriage does not guarantee a problem-free relationship. Marriage is a *human* institution, and humans are fallible. Even the most devout couples may face challenges and conflicts. However, the belief in God's presence can guide them towards forgiveness, understanding, and reconciliation. The teachings of many religious traditions emphasize the importance of forgiveness, and the power of love to heal wounds. In seeking God's guidance, couples can find the strength to *forgive* and move forward, fostering a stronger bond built on compassion and understanding.

Day 17

Finding Balance

Love, undoubtedly beautiful and rewarding, can also be a source of tremendous struggle, and subsequent growth. As the demands of work, personal life, and our love for each other grow, we are on a quest to achieve harmony in this delicate dance.

In the pursuit of professional success, we have found ourselves deeply invested in our careers. While it is fulfilling to see our hard work pay off, we have also recognized the need to create boundaries and prioritize quality time together. It is not always easy to strike a balance, but we are committed to making it work. Furthermore, we have come to embrace the beauty of *flexibility*. Life can be unpredictable, and sometimes our plans need to adjust accordingly. Instead of letting change disrupt us, we have learned to adapt and make the best out of every situation, even if it means altering our schedules to accommodate unforeseen circumstances.

As we continue to grow and evolve, we know that the pursuit of balance is an *ongoing* process. There will be days when it feels effortless, and others when it requires significant conscious effort. Nevertheless, we are committed to supporting each other on this journey, and staying steadfast in our love.

Firstly, self-love is the foundation upon which all other forms of love are built. It involves recognizing and valuing one's own worth, acknowledging strengths and weaknesses, and prioritizing personal well-being. Without a healthy sense of self-love, it becomes difficult to truly love others.

Self-love allows individuals to establish boundaries, practice self-care, and foster personal growth. By nurturing oneself, individuals can develop a keen sense of identity, making them more capable of offering love to others in a balanced and genuine manner.

Finding a balance between self-love, love for others, and love for the world is an ongoing process that requires self-reflection, self-awareness, and constant growth. It involves understanding that love is not a zero-sum game, and that by nurturing ourselves, we become better equipped to love and support those around us. It is about recognizing the importance of setting healthy boundaries, practicing self-care, and cultivating meaningful connections with others. It is also about extending our love *beyond* ourselves and embracing the beauty of the world we live in.

As the months went by, we discovered the power of shared experiences. Traveling together provided us with unforgettable memories and deepened our bond. Each adventure strengthened our connection, leaving us eager for *more* journeys ahead!

Among the milestones, the most significant was moving into our first home. Turning a house into a place filled with love, laughter, and warmth was a heartwarming process. We learned how to cooperate in creating a space that reflected both our personalities, making it truly our own. Throughout this year, we have grown both individually—and as a couple. We have learned to appreciate each other's quirks and unique qualities. We supported one another during challenging times—and celebrated each other's victories—with genuine pride.

Day 18

Putting in the Work

In our marriage, I have come to realize that love takes work—*constant* effort and communication, to keep the connection strong. We face challenges and disagreements, but through open and honest conversations, we find resolutions and grow together. Love is also about appreciating the trivial things, the everyday moments that make our bond stronger. From sharing laughter to supporting each other's dreams, the simple acts of kindness build a foundation of love and trust. As we navigate through the difficulties of life, I am grateful for the opportunities we have to learn and grow together. Each day, we discover new sides of ourselves and our relationship, reminding us that love is a *journey*, not a *destination*.

Relationships, whether romantic or platonic, require constant attention and understanding. They demand open communication, empathy, and compromise. It is through these efforts that two individuals can grow together and build a foundation of love and trust. By actively listening to one another, expressing emotions honestly, and trying to meet each other's needs, we create a safe and secure space for love to thrive.

Putting in the work for love also extends beyond the boundaries of individual relationships. Love has the power to create positive change on a larger scale. It calls on us to be compassionate and understanding towards others, even in the face of differences. By prioritizing love and connecting with others on a deeper level, we can foster a sense of unity. Love cannot simply be passive; it demands active participation and continuous nurturing. By putting in the work for love, we can ensure that it grows stronger and more resilient.

Day 19

Treasure Behind Love

It requires effort, communication, and a willingness to listen and understand. It demands compromise and empathy—learning to see the world through the lens of our beloved. In its truest form, love is unconditional. It does not look to own or control, but celebrates the freedom of the beloved, supporting their dreams and aspirations. Love is a profound journey of discovery, as we unravel the layers of our hearts and souls together, hand in hand, exploring the depths of emotion and connection.

As we embark on this journey of love, let us remember that love is not confined to romantic relationships alone. It extends to friends, family, and even strangers, for love knows no boundaries. In the end, love is a sacred dance of two souls entwined, two hearts beating in the labyrinth of life together, creating a melody that echoes throughout eternity. It is a treasure to be cherished, nurtured, and celebrated—for in love, we find the true essence of what it means to be *human*.

One of the treasures found in love is the profound sense of belonging and connection it brings. When we experience love, we feel a deep *connection* to another person, as if they are an extension of ourselves. It is this connection that allows us to truly understand and accept one another, overlooking flaws and imperfections. Love creates a cushion of support and understanding, allowing us to feel secure and safe in the presence of those we love.

Another treasure behind love is the happiness and joy it brings into our lives. Love has the power to uplift our spirits, bringing smiles to our faces and laughter to our hearts.

Love also teaches us valuable lessons about empathy, compassion, and forgiveness. It helps us develop a deeper understanding of ourselves and others, allowing us to appreciate the unique experiences and perspectives that each person brings to our lives. Love teaches us to look beyond our own needs and desires—encouraging us to be selfless and understanding about the feelings and emotions of others. The treasure behind love lies in its ability to bring fulfillment and a powerful sense of *purpose* to our lives. Love gives us a reason to live, to strive for happiness, and to make a positive impact on the world around us.

Day 20

Love Milestones

Love is a pathway, a winding road that often leads us through unexpected twists and turns, challenging us to grow and evolve. Along this path, there are countless milestones that mark our progress and shape our relationships. These love milestones are not just momentous events; they are *defining* moments that shift the dynamics of our love's story, and deepen our connection with our partner.

One of the first love milestones in any relationship is the spark of attraction. It is that magical moment when two souls collide, and fireworks ignite. It could happen in a crowded room, across a café, or even online. In that split second, time stands still, and two individuals are drawn to each other like magnets. This first attraction sets the stage for what is to come—a unique bond that holds the potential for lifelong love.

- The First "I Love You": Saying those three little words for the first time was a defining moment in our relationship. The trust, and the overwhelming joy of being loved and loving someone unconditionally became a cherished memory.

- Overcoming Obstacles: Life threw challenges our way, testing the strength of our love. Together, we faced these obstacles, providing unwavering support and encouragement. Each triumph made us realize that we were a team, capable of conquering anything together.

- Building Trust: Trust is the cornerstone of any relationship, and we worked tirelessly to build and nurture it. Open communication, honesty, and vulnerability allowed us to create a safe space where we could share our deepest fears and dreams.

- The First Fight and Reconciliation: Our first disagreement was scary, but it taught us the importance of healthy conflict resolution. We learned to listen, understand, and forgive, strengthening the bond between us.

Love milestones are the markers that shape our relationships. They symbolize growth, commitment, and the ability to overcome challenges together. These milestones show us that love is a lifelong journey filled with joy, pain, and everything in between. As we reach each milestone, our love deepens, and we become intertwined in the beautiful tapestry of love and companionship.

Day 91

Trust

I want to reflect on the importance of *communication* and *trust* in our relationship. These two love languages have been the foundation of our bond, strengthening our connection and creating a space where we can truly understand and support each other.

Communication has been our guiding light, allowing us to openly express our feelings, thoughts, and desires without fear of judgment. Through our heartfelt conversations, we have grown closer and learned how to navigate life's challenges together, hand in hand.

Trust, oh how it has blossomed between us! It is the unwavering belief in each other's intentions and actions that has fostered an environment of safety and security. Trusting you completely has given me the courage to be vulnerable and authentic, knowing that my heart is safe.

One of the main reasons why trust is so important in a relationship is because it builds a keen sense of emotional intimacy. When trust is present, individuals feel safe to reveal their true selves and let down their guards. This, in turn, fosters a deeper connection between partners, friends, or family members. Trust allows individuals to be seen, understood, and accepted for who they are, creating a strong bond of love and support.

Trust also plays a significant role in fostering personal growth and development. When individuals feel trusted and valued, they are more likely to take risks, explore new experiences, and reach their full potential. In a trusting relationship, partners, friends, or family members are encouraged to pursue their own passions and goals, knowing that they have a reliable support system by their side. This sense of trust empowers individuals to embrace their authentic selves and pursue personal growth—without fear of judgment or abandonment.

Day 22

Worthy of Love

Through the difficulties of relationships, I have learned so much about myself—my strengths, weaknesses, and areas for growth. Love has served as a mirror, reflecting the person I am, and the person I want to become. In the embrace of love, I have found acceptance and appreciation for my true self. It has taught me to be kinder to myself, embracing my imperfections and celebrating my unique qualities. Love has encouraged me to let go of self-doubt and insecurities, realizing that I am worthy of love and affection *just as I am*.

Love has been a catalyst for personal growth. It has challenged me to confront my fears, communicate my needs, and learn to compromise. Love has pushed me out of my comfort zone, encouraging me to take risks and pursue my passions. I am grateful for the lessons it has taught me.

Love has been a transformative force, shaping me into a better version of myself. I cherish the growth, the joy, and, yes, even the pain, for they have all contributed to the person I am today. Yet, in a world where superficiality, judgment, and perfectionism so often reign, it can be challenging to believe that we are truly *worthy* of love. However, every person—regardless of their background, struggles, or imperfections—is inherently worthy of love.

When we recognize and embrace our own essential worth, we create a solid foundation for self-acceptance, self-esteem, and self-care. We cultivate a sense of inner security and confidence that allows us to navigate through life's challenges. With love as our anchor, we become more resilient, compassionate, and generous individuals.

Worthiness of love is deeply rooted in our inherent value as human individuals. Each person is unique and has a multitude of qualities, talents, and strengths. We are far more than the sum of our mistakes, failures, or limitations. When we recognize and appreciate our own self-worth, we open ourselves up to receiving love from others. It is only when we believe in our own worthiness that we can fully embrace the love that is offered to us.

Let us remember that we are all worthy of love, and let us extend love to ourselves and others, knowing that it is a gift that knows *no* boundaries.

Day 93

Embracing the Journey

In our lifetime's journey, we will encounter several kinds of love—romantic love, familial love, and platonic love, among others. Each form of love offers its own unique lessons and blessings. Romantic love, for instance, teaches us about trust, communication, and compromise. It allows us to understand that love requires effort and commitment. Familial love teaches us about unconditional support, forgiveness, and the importance of kinship. Platonic love helps us appreciate the beauty of friendship and the power of emotional connection.

Embracing the journey of love requires an open heart and a willingness to take risks. It is about stepping outside of our comfort zones and allowing ourselves to be vulnerable. Love can be scary and uncertain, but it is through these challenges that we grow and evolve as individuals. When we let go of fear and embrace the journey, we give ourselves the opportunity to experience the depths of love and all its wonders.

Through the mirror of love, we see our strengths and weaknesses, our desires, and insecurities. It allows us to discover our own capacity to love and be loved. The journey may bring out our deepest fears and insecurities, but it also provides wonderful opportunities for growth and self-improvement. When we embrace love, we reveal our own potential—and learn to love ourselves more deeply.

The truth of the matter is that the journey of love is not always smooth. It is important to recognize and accept the challenges that come our way. Love is not without its trials; it tests our resilience, patience, and perseverance.

Relationships can face hardships, and heartbreaks may occur, but it is in those times that we learn the most about ourselves, and about love. The journey of love asks us to face these challenges head-on—and learn from them—rather than shy away, or run from them. It is in the face of adversity that true growth and transformation take place.

By opening our hearts and embracing the challenges and lessons that come our way, we can travel along the path of love with grace, and find lasting happiness.

So, let us embark on this beautiful journey God has laid out before us.

Day 24

How you Fight the Love Battles

Love can be a battleground, a fierce arena where emotions clash and hearts are at stake. It can be a beautiful and exhilarating feeling that has the power to overcome all obstacles, but it also has the potential to bring pain and heartbreak. In our journey to find—and maintain—love, we often find ourselves fighting battles that test our resilience, patience, and courage.

One of the most prominent battles in the pursuit of love is the battle against fear. Fear can be a powerful restraint, preventing us from fully opening our hearts and showing vulnerability. It can be terrifying to let someone into our lives, exposing ourselves to the possibility of rejection and hurt. However, it is in this battle that we must find the strength to overcome our fears, to take a leap of faith and trust that love will be *worth* the risk. It is in fighting the battle against fear that we discover our true capacity for love and connection.

Another fierce battle in the realm of love is the battle against societal expectations. Society often has preconceived notions and expectations about how love *should* look, and what relationships *should* be like. These expectations can lead us to doubt our own desires and suppress our true emotions. Fighting this battle means bravely embracing our own unique journey, rejecting societal pressure, and following our hearts, without apology. It is in defying societal norms that we find the freedom to love authentically and create relationships that are true to our own values and needs.

The battle to maintain love can also be a challenging one. Relationships require constant effort, compromise, and understanding. Inevitably, conflicts will arise, and it is in these heated moments that we must summon all our strength to fight for the love we have built. We must learn to communicate effectively, to listen with empathy, and to seek resolution even when it feels impossible.

The commitment to fight for love, no matter the obstacles, is what separates mediocre relationships from extraordinary ones. The most difficult battle of all is the battle within us. In our pursuit of love, we often come face to face with our own insecurities, fears, and flaws. We must confront our own demons, heal from past wounds, and work on personal growth. This inner battle is a crucial step towards becoming the best version of us and attracting healthy, fulfilling relationships. It is in fighting the battle within that we create space for love to flourish.

Despite the challenges and battles that love presents, it is a battle *worth* fighting. Love, in all its intricacies and complexities, is what gives life meaning and purpose. It has the power to heal, to transform, and to bring joy beyond measure. It is through these battles that we become warriors, armed with the knowledge that love is *worth* fighting for.

It is Written.

There is a belief that love is preordained by a higher power, by God. This notion suggests that every person has a soulmate, someone with whom they are destined to spend the rest of their lives. This idea of destined love has been celebrated and embraced throughout the ages in diverse cultures and religions. It brings a sense of comfort, hope, and purpose to those who believe in it. One of the foundations for this belief lies in the scripture itself. Many religious texts talk about love as a Divine gift, something that is created and guided by God. For example, in the Bible, it says, "He who finds a wife finds a good thing and obtains favor from the LORD" (Proverbs 18:22). This verse suggests that finding a partner is not a mere coincidence, but rather a blessing from God. It instills the belief that love can be a covenant—a sacred bond that is guided by a higher power. Furthermore, the concept of destined love is reinforced through the idea of soulmates. The notion that there is one person meant for another is widespread in various cultures.

This belief asserts that God has created an individual's perfect match, someone who complements and completes them. It is rooted in the idea that two souls are interconnected, and their paths are destined to cross. This conviction resonates with individuals who long for a deep and fulfilling connection with a partner. It provides solace in knowing that true love is out there, waiting to be discovered. Destined love by God also carries an element of faith. It requires individuals to have trust and belief in a Divine plan.

The journey to find true love can be challenging and filled with obstacles, but those who have faith in God's plan understand that these hurdles are a test of their commitment and perseverance. They perceive their romantic encounters, whether positive or negative, as steppingstones towards their destined love. This faith brings a sense of peace and comfort in knowing that God is guiding and orchestrating their love story.

It is written, that the love destined by God is not just about finding a partner, but also about cultivating a strong and loving relationship. It encourages individuals to love and support their partners *unconditionally*. It emphasizes the importance of treating one another with respect, kindness, and forgiveness. From a religious perspective, this love is seen as an expression of one's faith and devotion to God. It serves as a reminder of God's love for humanity and the importance of reflecting that love, However, it is essential to recognize that not everyone subscribes to the belief in destined love by God. Love is a complex and multifaceted emotion that can be influenced by many factors such as personal choices, compatibility, and timing. While some may find comfort in the belief in destined love, others may view love blossoms due to personal efforts and compatibility.

My Oath of Love

Love, a profound and complex emotion, holds *immense* power in our lives. It can ignite a fire within us, to bring us immeasurable joy and happiness, as well as to test our limits and challenge our very being. Love, in its truest form, demands dedication, selflessness, and an unbreakable connection. As I embark on this journey of love, I find myself contemplating my Oath of Love, the promises I make, and the intentions I hold dear.

Primarily, my Oath of Love is a commitment to wholeheartedly embrace love in all its rawness, imperfections, and uncertainties. Love is not always easy, nor does it always follow a smooth path. It is in accepting and cherishing the flaws and quirks of my beloved that I am truly able to experience authentic love. I vow to never try to change my partner into someone they are not, but instead to love and support them as they are, with all their strengths and weaknesses.

Furthermore, my Oath of Love encompasses a promise to be a pillar of strength and support in my partner's life. Love is not just about experiencing happiness together, but also about being there during the dark and tough times. I pledge to lend an empathetic ear, providing solace and guidance when needed. I will strive to be a source of encouragement, helping my partner navigate through the challenges of life, hand in hand.

In addition, my Oath of Love is rooted in a commitment to growth and self-improvement. Love has the power to inspire us to become better versions of ourselves. I vow to constantly work on my own personal and emotional growth, nurturing the love within myself—because when we love ourselves, we have more love to offer others. In turn, I promise to support and encourage my partner's aspirations and dreams, helping them become the best version of *themselves*.

Moreover, my Oath of Love entails a pledge to prioritize open and honest communication. Effective communication is the foundation of a healthy and thriving relationship. I promise to create an environment where my partner feels comfortable expressing their thoughts, fears, and desires. Without judgment or criticism, I will actively listen and provide honest feedback, fostering a space of love and understanding.

Finally, my Oath of Love includes a vow to never take my partner for granted. Love requires constant effort and appreciation. I will remind myself daily of the incredible privilege it is to be loved and to love unconditionally. I will treasure every moment, big or small, and express my gratitude for my partner's presence in my life. I will never allow complacency or routine to dull the flames of love, but instead, work to keep our bond strong and vibrant.

In conclusion, my Oath of Love is a testament to the *profound* commitment I am willing to make. It is a promise to embrace love in all its facets, to support and nurture my partner, to continually grow together, to communicate honestly and openly, and to *never* take our love for granted. Love, with all its complexities, is a gift that deserves to be cherished and nurtured. And with my oath of love, I am ready to embark on a journey of pure and enduring love.

A Daily Marriage Prayer

Lord, let my spouse's lips speak no evil and tongue speak no lies. Above all let us love each other deeply because love covers a multitude of (sin) faults. Father, make our marriage a blessing to us. Teach us to be kind to one another, tender-hearted, and forgiving one another as you have forgiven us.

Lord, let me and my spouse grow in grace and knowledge of Jesus Christ daily. Be with my spouse so they will succeed in everything they do. Help us to walk before you faithfully, with integrity of heart and uprightness.

Marriage Scriptures

The Blessing of Marriage

Photo by Alfonso Lorenzetto on Unsplash

Genesis 2:18 (NIV)
"The Lord God said, 'It is not good for the man to be alone. I will make a helper suitable for him.'"

Proverbs 18:22 (NIV)
"He who finds a wife finds what is good and receives favor from the Lord."

Matthew 19:6 (NIV)
"So they are no longer two, but one flesh. Therefore what God has joined together, let no one separate."

Ecclesiastes 4:9-10(ESV)

"Two are better than one, because they have a good return for their labor: If either of them falls down, one can help the other up. But pity anyone who falls and has no one to help them up."

Love and Friendship

Photo by Tyler Nix on Unsplash

1 Corinthians 13:4-7 (ESV)
"Love is patient and kind; love does not envy or boast; it is not arrogant or rude. It does not insist on its own way; it is not irritable or resentful; it does not rejoice at wrongdoing, but rejoices with the truth. Love bears all things, believes all things, hopes all things, endures all things"

Romans 12:10(ESV)
"Love one another with brotherly affection. Outdo one another in showing honor"

1 John 4:16 (ESV)
"We know and rely on the love God has for us. God is love. Whoever lives in love lives in God, and God in them"

Humility and Gentleness

Photo by Chermiti Mohamed on Unsplash

Ephesians 4:1-3(NIV)
"I urge you to live a life worthy of the calling you have received. Be completely humble and gentle; be patient, bearing with one another in love. Make every effort to keep the unity of the Spirit through the bond of peace"

Philippians 2:1-5 (ESV)
"So if there is any encouragement in Christ, any comfort from love, any participation in the Spirit, any affection and sympathy, complete my joy by being of the same mind, having the same love, being in full accord and of one mind. Do nothing from selfish ambition or conceit, but in humility count others more significant than yourselves. Let each of you look not only to his own interests, but also to the interests of others. Have this mind among yourselves, which is yours in Christ Jesus"

Compassion and Forgiveness

Photo by Victoria Roman on Unsplash

Ephesians 4:32(NIV)
And be ye kind one to another, tenderhearted, forgiving one another, even as God for Christ's sake hath forgiven you.

2 Peter 3:18 (NIV)
But grow in grace, and in the knowledge of our Lord and Saviour Jesus Christ. To him be glory both now and for ever. Amen.

Ephesians 5:25 (NIV)
"Husbands, love your wives, just as Christ loved the church and gave himself up for her."

Colossians 3:14 (NIV)
"And over all these virtues put on love, which binds them all together in perfect unity."

1Thessalonians 5:11(NIV)
"Therefore encourage one another and build each other up, just as in fact you are doing."

1 Corinthians 16:14 (NIV)
"Do everything in love."

Ephesians 4:32(NIV)
"Be kind and compassionate to one another, forgiving each other, just as in Christ God forgave you."

Colossians 3:12-13 (NIV)
"Therefore, as God's chosen people, holy and dearly loved, clothe yourselves with compassion, kindness, humility, gentleness and patience. Bear with each other and forgive one another if any of you has a grievance against someone. Forgive as the Lord forgave you"

Enthusiasm and Sentiment

Photo by Gama. Films on Unsplash

1 Corinthains 7:9(ESV)
"But if they cannot exercise self-control, they should marry. For it is better to marry than to burn with passion"

1 Peter 4:8(ESV)
"Above all, keep loving one another earnestly, since love covers a multitude of sins"

Faithfulness

Photo by Caroline Veronez on Unsplash

Hebrews 13:4(NIV)
"Marriage should be honored by all, and the marriage bed kept pure, for God will judge the adulterer and all the sexually immoral"

Proverbs 6:32(ESV)
"He who commits adultery lacks sense; he who does it destroys himself"

Guidance for Husbands and Wives

Photo by Justin Follis on Unsplash

1 Peter 3:7(NIV)
"Husbands, in the same way be considerate as you live with your wives, and treat them with respect as the weaker partner and as heirs with you of the gracious gift of life, so that nothing will hinder your prayers"

Proverbs 12:4(NIV)
"A wife of noble character is her husband's crown, but a disgraceful wife is like decay in his bones"

"Submit to one another out of reverence for Christ. Wives, submit yourselves to your own husbands as you do to the Lord. For the husband is the head of the wife as Christ is the head of the church, His body, of which

He is the Savior. Now as the church submits to Christ, so also wives should submit to their husbands in everything.

Ephesians 5:21-33
"Husbands, love your wives, just as Christ loved the church and gave Himself up for her to make her holy, cleansing her by the washing with water through the word, and to present her to Himself as a radiant church, without stain or wrinkle or any other blemish, but holy and blameless. In this same way, husbands ought to love their wives as their own bodies. He who loves his wife loves himself. After all, no one ever hated their own body, but they feed and care for their body, just as Christ does the church — for we are members of His body. 'For this reason a man will leave his father and mother and be united to his wife, and the two will become one flesh.' This is a profound mystery — but I am talking about Christ and the church. However, each one of you also must love his wife as he loves himself, and the wife must respect her husband"

Reflections!!

About the Author(s)

The recently weds Omar and Magan Parsons have a strong love for God. Jeremiah and A'mari Huntley are their two sons. They currently live in Diberville, Mississippi. Omar is from Mobile, Alabama. He currently works for Airbus as a Structural Assembler. Hattiesburg, Mississippi, is Magan's hometown. She holds licenses as a minister, cosmetologist, cosmetology instructor, and massage therapist. Both of them demonstrate a genuine desire to serve and assist others. The goal of writing this book was to encourage and support the mend of broken marriages and relationships. With God at the core of your ongoing relationship or marriage, healing and renewal are possible for all aspects. The Oath of Love provides avenues and diverse methods for expressing and understanding each other, but above all, it emphasizes the significance of appreciating one another. They hope that this book will offer you hope and enable you to experience love on a deeper level.

www.ingramcontent.com/pod-product-compliance
Lightning Source LLC
LaVergne TN
LVHW091535070526
838199LV00001B/69